Does Prayer Change Things?

Crucial Questions booklets provide a quick introduction to definitive Christian truths. This expanding collection includes titles such as:

Who Is Jesus?

Can I Trust the Bible?

Does Prayer Change Things?

Can I Know God's Will?

How Should I Live in This World?

What Does It Mean to Be Born Again?

Can I Be Sure I'm Saved?

What Is Faith?

What Can I Do with My Guilt?

What Is the Trinity?

TO BROWSE THE REST OF THE SERIES, PLEASE VISIT: **LIGONIER.ORG/CQ**

CQ

Does Prayer Change Things?

R.C. SPROUL

 LIGONIER MINISTRIES

Does Prayer Change Things?
© 2009 by R.C. Sproul

Previously published as *Effective Prayer* (1984) and as part of *Following Christ* (1991) by Tyndale House Publishers, and as *Does Prayer Change Things?* by Ligonier Ministries (1999).

Published by Ligonier Ministries
421 Ligonier Court, Sanford, FL 32771
Ligonier.org

Printed in China
RR Donnelley
0001121
First edition, fifteenth printing

ISBN 978-1-64289-038-9 (Paperback)
ISBN 978-1-64289-066-2 (ePub)
ISBN 978-1-64289-094-5 (Kindle)

Cover design: Ligonier Creative
Interior typeset: Katherine Lloyd, The DESK

Unless otherwise noted, Scripture quotations are from the ESV® Bible (The Holy Bible, English Standard Version®), copyright © 2001 by Crossway, a publishing ministry of Good News Publishers. Used by permission. All rights reserved.

Scripture quotations marked KJV are from the King James Version. Public domain.

The Library of Congress has cataloged the Reformation Trust edition as follows:
Sproul, R.C. (Robert Charles), 1939-2017
  [Effective prayer]
  Does prayer change things? / R.C. Sproul.
    p. cm. -- (The crucial questions series)
  First published as: Effective prayer, 1984. Following Christ. Wheaton, Ill. : Tyndale House Publishers, 1992. Does prayer change things? Ligonier Ministries, 1999.
  ISBN 978-1-56769-178-8
  1. Prayer--Christianity. I. Sproul, R.C. (Robert Charles), 1939- Following Christ. II. Title.
  BV220.S68 2009
  248.3'2--dc22
                                                2009018823

Contents

Chapter One

The Place
of Prayer

W hat is the goal of the Christian life? It is godliness
born of obedience to Christ. Obedience unlocks
the riches of the Christian experience. Prayer prompts
and nurtures obedience, putting the heart into the proper
"frame of mind" to desire obedience.

Of course, knowledge is also important because without it we cannot know what God requires. However,
knowledge and truth remain abstract unless we commune
with God in prayer. The Holy Spirit teaches, inspires, and

illumines God's Word to us. He mediates the Word of God and assists us in responding to the Father in prayer.

Simply put, prayer has a vital place in the life of the Christian. One might pray and not be a Christian, but one cannot be a Christian and not pray. Romans 8:15 tells us that the spiritual adoption that has made us sons of God causes us to cry out in verbal expressions: "Abba! Father!" Prayer is to the Christian what breath is to life, yet no duty of the Christian is so neglected.

Prayer, at least private prayer, is difficult to do out of a false motive. One can preach out of a false motive, as do the false prophets. One can be involved in Christian activities out of false motives. Many of the externals of religion can be done from false motives. However, it is highly unlikely that anyone would commune with God out of some improper motive.

We are invited, even commanded, to pray. Prayer is both a privilege and a duty, and any duty can become laborious. Prayer, like any means of growth for the Christian, requires work. In a sense, prayer is unnatural to us. Though we were created for fellowship and communion with God, the effects of the fall have left most of us lazy and indifferent toward something as important as prayer. Rebirth quickens a new desire for communion with God, but sin resists the Spirit.

We can take comfort from the fact that God knows our hearts and hears our unspoken petitions as well as the words that emanate from our lips. Whenever we are unable to express the deep feelings and emotions of our souls or when we are completely unclear about what we ought to be praying, the Holy Spirit intercedes for us. Romans 8:26–27 says: "The Spirit helps us in our weakness. For we do not know what to pray for as we ought, but the Spirit himself intercedes for us with groanings too deep for words. And he who searches hearts knows what is the mind of the Spirit, because the Spirit intercedes for the saints according to the will of God." When we don't know how to pray or what to pray for in a given situation, the Holy Spirit assists us. There is reason to believe from the text that if we pray incorrectly, the Holy Spirit corrects the errors in our prayers before He takes them before the Father, for verse 27 tells us that He "intercedes for the saints according to the will of God."

Prayer is the secret of holiness—if holiness, indeed, has anything secretive about it. If we examine the lives of the great saints of the church, we find that they were great people of prayer. John Wesley once remarked that he didn't think much of ministers who didn't spend at least four hours per day in prayer. Luther said that he prayed regularly for an hour every day except when he experienced a particularly busy day. Then he prayed for two hours.

The neglect of prayer is a major cause of stagnation in the Christian life. Consider the example of Peter in Luke 22:39–62. Jesus went to the Mount of Olives to pray, as was His custom, and told His disciples, "Pray that you may not enter into temptation." The disciples fell asleep instead. The next thing Peter did was try to take on the Roman army with a sword; then he denied Christ. Peter did not pray, and as a result he fell into temptation. What is true of Peter is true of all of us: we fall in private before we ever fall in public.

Is there a right and wrong time for prayer? Isaiah 50:4 talks about the morning as the time when God gives the desire to pray on a daily basis. But other passages give times of prayer during all hours of the day. No part of the day is set apart as more sanctified than another. Jesus prayed in the morning, during the day, and sometimes all night long. There is evidence that He had a time set aside for prayer; however, considering the relationship Jesus had with the Father, we know that communion between them never stopped.

First Thessalonians 5:17 commands us to pray without ceasing. This means that we are to be in a continual state of communion with our Father.

Prayer, then, is central and crucial in the life of the Christian. Let us look further into this vital but neglected and misunderstood Christian discipline.

Chapter Two

The Purpose of Prayer

Nothing escapes God's notice; nothing oversteps the boundaries of His power. God is authoritative in all things. If I thought even for one moment that a single molecule were running loose in the universe outside the control and domain of almighty God, I wouldn't sleep tonight. My confidence in the future rests in my confidence in the God who controls history. But how does God exercise that control and manifest that authority? How does God bring to pass the things He sovereignly decrees?

Augustine said that nothing happens in this universe apart from the will of God and that, in a certain sense, God ordains everything that happens. Augustine was not attempting to absolve men of responsibility for their actions, but his teaching raises a question: If God is sovereign over the actions and intents of men, why pray at all? A secondary concern revolves around the question, "Does prayer really change anything?"

Let me answer the first question by stating that the sovereign God commands by His holy Word that we pray. Prayer is not optional for the Christian; it is required.

We might ask, "What if it doesn't do anything?" That is not the issue. Regardless of whether prayer does any good, if God commands us to pray, we must pray. It is reason enough that the Lord God of the universe, the Creator and Sustainer of all things, commands it. Yet He not only commands us to pray, but also invites us to make our requests known. James says that we have not because we ask not (James 4:2). He also tells us that the prayer of a righteous man accomplishes much (James 5:16). Time and again the Bible says that prayer is an effective tool. It is useful; it works.

John Calvin, in the *Institutes of the Christian Religion,* makes some profound observations regarding prayer:

But, someone will say, does God not know, even without being reminded, both in what respect we are troubled and what is expedient for us, so that it may seem in a sense superfluous that he should be stirred up by our prayers—as if he were drowsily blinking or even sleeping until he is aroused by our voice? But they who thus reason do not observe to what end the Lord instructed his people to pray, for he ordained it not so much for his own sake as for ours. Now he wills—as is right—that his due be rendered to him, in the recognition that everything men desire and account conducive to their own profit comes from him, and in the attestation of this by prayers. But the profit of this sacrifice also, by which he is worshiped, returns to us. Accordingly, the holy fathers, the more confidently they extolled God's benefits among themselves and others, were the more keenly aroused to pray . . .

Still it is very important for us to call upon him: First, that our hearts may be fired with a zealous and burning desire ever to seek, love, and serve him, while we become accustomed in every need to flee to him as to a sacred anchor. Secondly, that there may enter our hearts no desire and no wish at all of which we should be ashamed to make him a witness, while we learn to set all our wishes before his eyes, and even to pour out our whole hearts. Thirdly, that we be prepared to receive his benefits with true gratitude of heart and thanksgiving, benefits that our prayer reminds us come from his hand. (Calvin, *Institutes of the Christian Religion*, trans. Ford Lewis Battles, ed. John T. McNeill [Louisville: Westminster John Knox, 1960], Book 3, chapter 20, section 3.)

Prayer, like everything else in the Christian life, is for God's glory and for our benefit, in that order. Everything that God does, everything that God allows and ordains, is in the supreme sense for His glory. It is also true that while God seeks His own glory supremely, man benefits when God is glorified. We pray to glorify God, but we also pray in order to receive the benefits of prayer from His hand. Prayer is for our benefit, even in light of the fact that God knows the end from the beginning. It is our privilege to bring the whole of our finite existence into the glory of His infinite presence.

The Purpose of Prayer

A Discourse with God

One of the great themes of the Reformation was the idea that all of life is to be lived under the authority of God, to the glory of God, in the presence of God. Prayer is not simply a soliloquy, a mere exercise in therapeutic self-analysis, or a religious recitation. Prayer is discourse with the personal God Himself. There, in the act and dynamic of praying, I bring my whole life under His gaze. Yes, He knows what is in my mind, but I still have the privilege of articulating to Him what is there. He says: "Come. Speak to me. Make your requests known to me." So we come in order to know Him and to be known by Him.

There is something erroneous in the question, "If God knows everything, why pray?" The question assumes that prayer is one-dimensional and is defined simply as supplication or intercession. On the contrary, prayer is multidimensional. God's sovereignty casts no shadow over the prayer of adoration. God's foreknowledge or determinate counsel does not negate the prayer of praise. The only thing it should do is give us greater reason for expressing our adoration for who God is. If God knows what I'm going to say before I say it, His knowledge, rather than limiting my prayer, enhances the beauty of my praise.

My wife and I are as close as two people can be. Often I know what she's going to say almost before she says it. The reverse is also true. But I still like to hear her say what is on her mind. If that is true of man, how much more true is it of God? We have the matchless privilege of sharing our innermost thoughts with God. Of course, we could simply enter our prayer closets, let God read our minds, and call that prayer. But that's not communion and it's certainly not communication.

We are creatures who communicate primarily through speech. Spoken prayer is obviously a form of speech, a way for us to commune and communicate with God. There is a certain sense in which God's sovereignty should influence our attitude toward prayer, at least with respect to adoration. If anything, our understanding of God's sovereignty should provoke us to an intense prayer life of thanksgiving. Because of such knowledge, we should see that every benefit, every good and perfect gift, is an expression of the abundance of His grace. The more we understand God's sovereignty, the more our prayers will be filled with thanksgiving.

In what way could God's sovereignty *negatively* affect the prayer of contrition, of confession? Perhaps we could draw the conclusion that our sin is ultimately God's responsibility and that our confession is an accusation of guilt against God Himself. Every true Christian knows that he cannot blame God for his sin. I may not understand the relationship between divine sovereignty and human responsibility, but I do realize that what stems from the wickedness of my own heart may not be assigned to the will of God. So we must pray because we are guilty, pleading the pardon of the Holy One whom we have offended.

Does Prayer Change Anything?

But what about intercession and supplication? It's nice to talk about the religious, spiritual, and psychological benefits (and whatever else might derive from prayer), but what about the real question—Does prayer make any difference? Does it really change anything? Someone once asked me that question, only in a slightly different manner: "Does prayer change God's mind?" My answer brought storms of protest. I said simply, "No." Now, if the person had asked me, "Does prayer change things?" I would have answered, "Of course!"

The Bible says there are certain things God has decreed from all eternity. Those things will inevitably come to pass.

If you were to pray individually or if you and I were to join forces in prayer or if all the Christians of the world were to pray collectively, it would not change what God, in His hidden counsel, has determined to do. If we decided to pray for Jesus not to return, He still would return. You might ask, though, "Doesn't the Bible say that if two or three agree on anything, they'll get it?" Yes, it does, but that passage is talking about church discipline, not prayer requests. So we must take all the biblical teaching on prayer into account and not isolate one passage from the rest. We must approach the matter in light of the whole of Scripture, resisting an atomistic reading.

Again, you might ask, "Doesn't the Bible say from time to time that God repents?" Yes, the Old Testament certainly says so. The book of Jonah tells us that God "repented of" the judgment He had planned for the people of Nineveh (Jonah 3:10, KJV). In using the concept of repentance here, the Bible is describing God, who is Spirit, in what theologians call "anthropomorphic" language. Obviously the Bible does not mean that God repented in the way we would repent; otherwise, we could rightly assume that God had sinned and therefore would need a savior Himself. What it clearly means is that God removed the threat of judgment from the people. The Hebrew word *nacham,* translated "repent" in the King James Version, means "comforted" or "eased" in this case. God was comforted and felt at ease that the people had turned from their sin, and therefore He revoked the sentence of judgment He had imposed.

When God hangs His sword of judgment over people's heads, and they repent and He then withholds His judgment, has He really changed His mind?

The mind of God does not change for God does not change. *Things* change, and they change according to His sovereign will, which He exercises through secondary means and secondary activities. The prayer of His people is one of the means He uses to bring things to pass in this world. So if you ask me whether prayer changes things, I answer with an unhesitating "Yes!"

It is impossible to know how much of human history reflects God's immediate intervention and how much reveals God working through human agents. Calvin's favorite example of this was the book of Job. The Sabeans and the Chaldeans had taken Job's donkeys and camels. Why? Because Satan had stirred their hearts to do so. But why? Because Satan had received permission from God to test Job's faithfulness in any way he so desired, short of taking Job's life. Why had God agreed to such a thing? For three reasons: (1) to silence the slander of Satan; (2) to vindicate Himself; and (3) to vindicate Job from the slander of Satan. All of these reasons are perfectly righteous justifications for God's actions.

By contrast, Satan's purpose in stirring up these two groups was to cause Job to blaspheme God—an altogether wicked motive. But we notice that Satan did not do something supernatural to accomplish his ends. He chose human agents—the Sabeans and Chaldeans, who were evil by nature—to steal Job's animals. The Sabeans and Chaldeans were known for their thievery and murderous way of life. Their will was involved, but there was no coercion; God's purpose was accomplished through their wicked actions.

The Sabeans and Chaldeans were free to choose, but for them, as for us, freedom always means freedom within limits. We must not, however, confuse human freedom and human autonomy. There will always be a conflict between divine sovereignty and human autonomy. There is never a conflict between divine sovereignty and human freedom. The Bible says that man is free, but he is not an autonomous law unto himself.

Suppose the Sabeans and Chaldeans had prayed, "Lead us

not into temptation, but deliver us from the evil one." I'm absolutely certain that Job's animals still would have been stolen, but not necessarily by the Sabeans and Chaldeans. God might have chosen to answer their prayer, but He would have used some other agent to steal Job's animals. There is freedom within limits, and within those limits, our prayers can change things. The Scriptures tell us that Elijah, through prayer, kept the rain from falling. He was not dissuaded from praying by his understanding of divine sovereignty.

The Prayers of the Son of God

No human being has ever had a more profound understanding of divine sovereignty than Jesus. No man ever prayed more fiercely or more effectively. Even in Gethsemane, He requested an option, a different way. When the request was denied, He bowed to the Father's will. The very reason we pray is because of God's sovereignty, because we believe that God has it within His power to order things according to His purpose. That is what sovereignty is all about—ordering things according to God's purpose. So then, does prayer change God's mind? No. Does prayer change things? Yes, of course.

The promise of the Scriptures is that "The prayer of a righteous person has great power as it is working" (James 5:16). The problem is that we are not all that righteous. What prayer most often changes is the wickedness and the hardness of our own hearts. That alone would be reason enough to pray, even if none of the other reasons were valid or true.

In a sermon titled "The Most High, a Prayer-Hearing God," Jonathan Edwards gave two reasons why God requires prayer:

> With respect *to God*, prayer is but a sensible acknowledgement of our dependence on him to his glory. As he hath made all things for his own glory, so he will be glorified and acknowledged by his creatures; and it is fit that he should require this of those who would be subjects of his mercy . . . [it] is a suitable acknowledgement of our dependence on the power and mercy of God for that which we need, and but a suitable honor paid to the great Author and Fountain of all good.
>
> With respect *to ourselves*, God requires prayer of us . . . Fervent prayer many ways tends to prepare the heart. Hereby is excited a sense of our need . . .

whereby the mind is more prepared to prize [his mercy] . . . Our prayer to God may excite in us a suitable sense and consideration of our dependence on God for the mercy we ask, and a suitable exercise of faith in God's sufficiency, so that we may be prepared to glorify his name when the mercy is received. (*The Works of Jonathan Edwards* [Carlisle, Pa.: Banner of Truth Trust, 1974], 2:116)

All that God does is for His glory first and for our benefit second. We pray because God commands us to pray, because it glorifies Him, and because it benefits us.

Chapter Three

The Pattern of Prayer

Jesus performed many miracles. During the course of His ministry, He walked on water, turned water into wine, healed the sick, raised the dead. As John said, "There are also many other things that Jesus did. Were every one of them to be written, I suppose that the world itself could not contain the books that would be written" (John 21:25).

I have always been amazed that the disciples didn't ask Jesus how to walk on water, how to still the tempest, or how to do any of His other miracles. They did, however, ask Jesus to teach them about prayer. Note that they did not ask Jesus to teach them *how* to pray; instead they begged, "Teach us *to* pray" (Luke 11:1). I'm certain that the disciples clearly saw the inseparable relationship between the power Jesus manifested and the hours He spent in solitude, conversing with His Father.

The instruction Jesus gives regarding prayer comes to us both from the Sermon on the Mount in Matthew 6 and from Luke 11. Jesus prefaces His remarks on the pattern for prayer with these words:

> "And when you pray, you must not be like the hypocrites. For they love to stand and pray in the synagogues and at the street corners, that they may be seen by others. Truly, I say to you, they have received their reward. But when you pray, go into your room and shut the door and pray to your Father who is in secret. And your Father who sees in secret will reward you.
>
> "And when you pray, do not heap up empty phrases as the Gentiles do, for they think that they will be heard for their many words. Do not be like them, for your Father knows what you need before you ask him. Pray then like this." (Matt. 6:5–9)

Notice that Jesus said, "Pray then like this," not "Pray this prayer" or "Pray these words." There is some question as to whether Jesus ever meant for us to repeat the prayer. I'm not attacking the use of the Lord's Prayer; there's certainly nothing wrong with its use in the personal life of the believer or the devotional life of the church. Yet Jesus was not so much giving us a prayer to recite as a pattern to show us the way in which to pray. Jesus was providing us with an outline of priorities or those things that *ought* to be priorities in our prayer lives. Let's look at the sections of the Lord's Prayer one at a time.

Our Father

The first two words of the prayer are radical as used in the New Testament. The word Father was not the basic form of address for God found in the old covenant community. His name was ineffable; He was not to be addressed with any degree of intimacy. The term *Father* was almost never used to speak of God or to address Him in prayer in the Old Testament. But in the New Testament, Jesus brought us into an intimate relationship with the Father, breaking down the partition symbolized by the veil in the temple.

Jesus gave us the incomparable privilege of calling God "Father."

Jesus was the first on record to take prayer and make it a personal discourse with God. Jesus, who spoke Aramaic, used the Aramaic word *Abba,* best translated "Dad" or "Papa." We can almost hear the cry of alarm from the disciples and see the looks of astonishment on their faces: "You don't mean it, Jesus. You can't be serious! We're not even allowed to speak the name of God aloud. We don't even call him *Father,* much less *Dad!*"

Ironically, today we live in a world that assumes God is the Father of everyone, that all men are brothers. We hear this in the cliches "the fatherhood of God" and "the brotherhood of man." But nowhere does Scripture say that all men are our brothers. It does say, however, that all men are our *neighbors.*

There is a restricted sense in which God is the Father of all men as the Giver and Sustainer of life, the *progenitor par excellence* of the human race. But nothing in the Bible indicates that an individual may approach God in a familiar sense. The only exception is when that person has been adopted into God's family, having expressed saving faith in the atonement of Christ and having submitted to His lordship. Then and only then is one afforded the privilege of calling God his Father. To those who received Him, God "gave the right [authority, privilege] to become children of God" (John 1:12). Only then does God call men "sons." The Greek word *exousia,* translated "right to become," denotes the freedom to act and the authority for that action. Calling God "Father" without the proper credential of sonship is an act of extreme presumption and arrogance.

We don't find the idea of universal fatherhood and brotherhood in the introduction to the Lord's Prayer. This cultural tacit assumption causes us to miss what Jesus is saying. In the first place, the fatherhood of God cannot be taken for granted by anyone in the world. Jesus is the one person with the ultimate right to address God in this way, for Jesus alone is the *monogenes,* "the only begotten of the Father" (John 1:14, KJV), having existed from all eternity in a unique filial relationship with the Father.

If there is a universal fatherhood and brotherhood in any sense whatsoever, it would have to be in the context of Jesus' discussion with the Pharisees in John 8. The Pharisees were claiming to be children of Abraham, offspring of God by ancestral association. Jesus challenged them on this point, saying, "If you were Abraham's children, you would be doing the works Abraham did, but now you seek to kill me, a man who has told you the truth that I heard from God. This is not what Abraham did . . . You are of your father the devil, and your will is to do your father's desires" (John 8:39–40, 44).

There is a clear distinction between the children of God and the children of the Devil. God's children hear His voice and obey Him. The children of the Devil do not listen to God's voice; they disobey Him by doing the will of their father, Satan. There are only two families, and everyone belongs to one or the other. Both groups have one thing in common, however. The members of each family do the will of their respective fathers, whether God or Satan.

If we go through the New Testament, making inquiry as to who are the sons of God, the answer is clear. The New Testament is neither vague nor enigmatic on this point. Romans 8:14–17a says this:

For all who are led by the Spirit of God are sons of God. For you did not receive the spirit of slavery to fall back into fear, but you received the Spirit of adoption as sons, by whom we cry, "Abba! Father."

The Spirit himself bears witness with our spirit that we are children of God, and if children, then heirs—heirs of God and fellow heirs with Christ.

In verse 14 of this passage, the word *all* (*autoi* in the Greek) is in what is called the *emphatic* form to indicate an exclusiveness. The verse is best translated, "For all who are being led by the Spirit of God, these *alone* are the sons of God" or "these *only* are the sons of God." Paul teaches that it is *only* by the Holy Spirit that we can call God our Father. The significance of this in the New Testament is that we are sons, not illegitimate children, because we are in union with Christ. Our sonship is not automatic; it is not inherited and it is not a genetic necessity, but rather it is derived. The New Testament word for this transaction is *adoption*. Because of our adoptive relationship with God through Christ, we become joint heirs with Christ.

It is only because we are in Christ and Christ is in us that we have the privilege of addressing God as our Father and of approaching Him in a filial relationship. Martin Luther once said that if he could just understand the first two words of the Lord's Prayer, he would never be the same again.

The word *our* signifies that the right to call God "Father" is not mine alone. It is a corporate privilege belonging to the entire body of Christ. When I pray, I do not come before God as an isolated individual, but as a member of a family, a community of saints.

In Heaven

At the time Jesus spoke the words of the Lord's Prayer, a debate was raging over the precise location of God's presence. In the discussion between Jesus and the woman at the well, Jesus was quick to point out that God is spirit, and as such could not be pinpointed to one particular place (John 4). He was neither at Mount Gerizim, as she thought, nor in Jerusalem, as some of the Jews believed.

To be sure, God is omnipresent. There are no finite restrictions to His divine presence, yet Christ spoke of the Father's being in heaven. Why? Christ was speaking about God's transcendence. Since God is not part of this worldly process, He is not part of nature. He cannot be confined to a locality. The God whom we address is above and beyond the finite limits of the world.

The opening line of the Lord's Prayer presents a dynamic tension for us. Although we are to come before the Lord in an attitude of intimacy, there is still an element of separation. We can come to God and call Him Father, but this filial relationship does not allow us to have the type of familiarity that breeds contempt. We are to come with boldness, yes, but never with arrogance or presumption. "Our Father" speaks of the nearness of God, but "in heaven" points to His otherness, His being set apart. The point is this: When we pray, we must remember who we are and whom we are addressing.

Hallowed Be Your Name

No matter how close God invites us to come, there is still an infinite gulf between our sinfulness and His majesty. He is the heavenly one; we are of the earth. He is perfect; we are imperfect. He is infinite; we are finite. He is holy; we are unholy. We must never forget that God is wholly "other" than we.

The sacred "otherness" of God is a fact the sons of Aaron forgot, but they forgot it only once. In Leviticus 10:1–3 we read:

> Now Nadab and Abihu, the sons of Aaron, each took his censer and put fire in it and laid incense on it and offered unauthorized fire before the LORD, which he had not commanded them. And fire came out from

before the LORD and consumed them, and they died before the LORD. Then Moses said to Aaron, "This is what the LORD has said, 'Among those who are near me I will be sanctified, and before all the people I will be glorified.'"

God demands to be treated as holy, for He is holy. He is jealous for His honor. He does not plead for respect in this passage. Rather, it is a statement of fact: "I will be treated as holy." We must never make the fatal mistake of Nadab and Abihu and approach the sovereign God in a flippantly casual attitude.

Looking at the first petition of the Lord's Prayer, we can see that this is the first priority of which Jesus spoke. His initial request was that the name of God be hallowed. It is the Greek word *hagios,* which is literally translated "holy." The top priority for the Christian is to see that God's name is kept holy, for it is holy. If that were the only prayer request the Christian community ever made, and if believers made it earnestly and regularly, I suspect the revival we pray for and the reformation we so earnestly desire would be accomplished in no time. Everything—our work, our ministry, and all aspects of our daily lives—would be affected.

In the Old Testament, the stated purpose for the Israelites' election and for their religious and dietary laws and ceremonies was to establish them as a holy nation, set apart from the commonplace cultures of antiquity. Was it for their honor? No, it was for *God's* honor. God's honor must become the obsession of the Christian community today. Honor must go not to our organizations, our denominations, our individual modes of worship, or even our particular churches, but to God alone.

Consider the words given in Ezekiel 36:22: "Thus says the Lord GOD: It is not for your sake, O house of Israel, that I am about to act, but for the sake of my holy name, which you have profaned among the nations to which you came." What a shift. The nation chosen to have the matchless privilege of showing forth the greatness of God had chosen to profane His name publicly. God had to rebuke them for their treason. In the final analysis, our names, our organizations, and our efforts are all meaningless unless we honor God's name.

Today a frightening lack of fear of God prevails in our world. Martin Luther once remarked that those around him spoke to God "as if He were a shoe clerk's apprentice." If that was true in Luther's day, how much more so today?

Yet the top priority that Jesus established is that the name of God should be hallowed, honored, and exalted.

God's name is an expression of who He is. We are the image-bearers of God. Where God is not respected, it is inevitable that His image-bearers will also suffer a loss of respect.

Your Kingdom Come

One central motif in the Scriptures is the kingdom of God. It was the main thrust of Jesus' teaching and preaching. Jesus came as the fulfillment of John the Baptist's message, which was clear, precise, and simple: "Repent, for the kingdom of heaven is at hand" (Matt. 3:2).

Jesus focused on the kingdom in the Sermon on the Mount, the keynote address of His preaching. Because of this focus, the sermon was more than simply an ethical presentation of principles for good living. Jesus was talking about the character traits of people who live a redeemed lifestyle within the kingdom of God.

The kingdom concept is difficult for American Christians to understand. Ours is a democracy, where the mere idea of a monarchy is repugnant. We are heirs of the revolutionaries who proclaimed, "We will serve no sovereign here!" Our nation is built on a resistance to sovereignty. Americans have fought battles and entire wars to be delivered from monarchy. How are we to understand the minds of New Testament people who were praying for the Son of David to restore a monarchy and the throne of Israel?

The King has come. Christ sits exalted at the right hand of God and reigns as King. But Jesus is not merely the spiritual King of the church, where His only responsibility is to exercise authority over our piety, as if there were a separation between church and state. Jesus is King of the universe. That is the fact of the ascension. This reality, however, is not believed or acknowledged by the world. Though that kingship is an established fact, it is *invisible* to the world in which we live. In heaven, there is no question about it. On the earth, there is considerable question about it. Jesus was saying that we must pray that the kingdom of God will become visible on the earth, that the invisible will be made visible.

Rebellion against God's authority is nothing new or unique to our day or to Western culture. In Psalm 2:2–3, we read: "The kings of the earth set themselves, and the rulers take counsel together, against the Lord and against his Anointed, saying, 'Let us burst their bonds apart and cast away their cords from us.'"

What is God's response to this uprising? "He who sits in the heavens laughs; the LORD holds them in derision" (Ps. 2:4). But God is not amused for long, for we read in verses 5–6, "Then he will speak to them in his wrath, and terrify them in his fury, saying, 'I have set my King on Zion, my holy hill.'"

The Lord speaks to those who have rebelled against Him—those involved in this cosmic Declaration of Independence—and declares, "I have installed my King, I have anointed my Christ, and you had better submit to Him." Reading further in verse 10, we learn something else:

> Now therefore, O kings, be wise; be warned, O rulers of the earth. Serve the LORD with fear, . . . lest he be angry, and you perish in the way, for his wrath is quickly kindled. Blessed are all who take refuge in him.

Christians are to pray for the manifestation of the reign of Christ and the emergence of His kingdom. If that is our prayer, it is our responsibility to show our allegiance to the King. People won't have to guess about whom we are exalting.

Your Will Be Done

This phrase is not asking that God's determinate counsel come to pass or that God usher in those things that He has foreordained from eternity. Rather, we are praying for obedience to the revealed preceptive will of God—what He has made plain to us by way of His commandments. This third petition is a prayer for obedience on the part of God's people, that those who are the people of God will obey the mandates of God.

On Earth As It Is in Heaven

The angels in God's court do as He says and desires. His people on earth do not. God is the Covenant Maker; we are the covenant breakers, frequently on a collision course with the will of the Father.

There is a sense in which the first three petitions are all saying the same thing. The honoring of God's name, the visibility of His kingdom, and the obedience to His will are virtually the same concept repeated three different ways. They are inseparably related. God is honored by our obedience, His kingdom is made visible by our obedience, and quite obviously His will is done when we are obedient to that will. These are the priorities Jesus laid down.

We should not come rushing into God's presence arrogantly, assaulting Him with our petty requests, forgetting whom we are addressing. We are to make certain we have properly exalted the God of creation. Only after God has been rightly honored, adored, and exalted do the subsequent petitions of God's people assume their proper place.

Give Us This Day Our Daily Bread

God provides for His people. It is noteworthy that the request here is for daily bread, not daily steak or daily prime rib. God provides the necessities, but not always the niceties.

Look at the experience of the Israelites after their deliverance from the land of Egypt. God miraculously provided the people with bread in the form of manna. Then what happened? First, they stopped thanking Him for His provision. Second, they stopped asking Him for His provision. Third, they began grumbling about His provision. Finally, they began reminiscing about how good things had been in Egypt. They dreamed about the cucumbers, the melons, the leeks, and the garlic they had had in Egypt—all the while forgetting about the oppression, the hardships, and the tortures they had endured at the hands of Pharaoh. They grumbled about having to eat manna for breakfast, manna for lunch, and manna for dinner. The Israelites ate manna soufflé, manna pie, manna meringue, boiled manna, baked manna, and broiled manna. Soon, they cried out for meat. The story is relayed to us in Numbers 11:18–20:

> Say to the people, "Consecrate yourselves for tomorrow, and you shall eat meat; for you have wept in the hearing of the LORD, saying, 'Who will give us meat to eat? For it was better for us in Egypt.' Therefore the LORD will give you meat, and you shall eat. You shall not eat just one day, or two days, or five days, or ten days, or twenty days, but a whole month, until it comes out at your nostrils and becomes loathsome to you."

God said, "If you want meat, I'll give you meat, and you're going to eat meat until you're sick of it."

One of the things that betrays our fallen condition is the concept of the self-made man, one who takes credit for the bounty of his goods and forgets the Source of all his provision. We must remember that God gives us all we have in the ultimate sense.

Forgive Us Our Debts, As We Also Have Forgiven Our Debtors

This is an extremely dangerous prayer to pray, but it contains a principle that the New Testament takes very seriously. The supreme warning from Jesus is that God will judge us according to how we have judged other people. Since man is saved by grace, what better evidence could there be of a man's salvation than that he offers to others the grace he himself has received? If such grace is not conspicuous in our lives, we may validly question the genuineness of our own alleged conversion.

We must take God seriously on this point. In Matthew 18:23–35, Jesus tells the story of two men who owed money. One owed roughly $10 million and the other owed about $18. The debt of the one who owed the large sum was forgiven by the man to whom he owed that debt. But he, in turn, would not forgive the man who owed him the paltry sum of $18.

Interestingly enough, both men asked for the same thing—more time, not a total release from the debt. It was comical for the man with the exorbitantly large debt to ask for more time, since even by today's wage standards the amount owed was an astronomical figure. The daily wage at that time was approximately eighteen cents. The man with the small debt could have paid his debt in three months. His request for more time was not unreasonable, but his creditor, rather than expressing the forgiveness he had received, began to harass him. The point should be clear. Our offenses to each other and the offenses people do to us are like an $18 debt, while the innumerable offenses we have committed against the Lord God are like the $10 million debt.

Jonathan Edwards, in his famous sermon "The Justice of God in the Damnation of Sinners," said that any sin is more or less heinous, depending on the honor and majesty of the one whom we have offended. Since God is of infinite honor, infinite majesty, and infinite holiness, the slightest sin is of infinite consequence. Such seemingly trivial sins are nothing less than "cosmic treason" when viewed in light of the great King against whom we have sinned. We are debtors who cannot pay, yet we have been released from the threat of debtors' prison. It is an insult to God for us to withhold forgiveness and grace from those who ask us, while claiming to be forgiven and saved by grace ourselves.

There is another important point to consider here. Even in our act of forgiveness there is no merit. We cannot commend ourselves to God and claim forgiveness merely because we have shown forgiveness to someone else. Our forgiveness in no way obligates God toward us. Luke 17:10 clearly points out that there is no merit even in the best of our good works: "When you have done all that you were commanded, say, 'We are unworthy servants; we have only done what was our duty.'"

We deserve nothing for our obedience, because obedience—even to the point of perfection—is the minimal requirement of a citizen of God's kingdom. Having done that duty, the only thing we could claim would be a lack of punishment, but certainly no reward, because we would have done only what was expected. Obedience never qualifies as service "above and beyond the call of duty." However, we have not obeyed; we have sinned grievously. Therefore, we are merely in a position to prostrate ourselves before God and beg for His forgiveness. But if we do, we must be prepared to show that forgiveness ourselves; otherwise our position in Christ dangles precariously. The bottom line of what Jesus is saying is this: "Forgiven people forgive other people." We dare not claim to be possessors of His life and nature and at the same time fail to exhibit that life and nature.

To carry the thought further, if God has forgiven someone, can we do any less? It would be incredible to think that we, who are so guilty, would refuse to forgive someone who has been forgiven by God, who is completely guiltless. We are to be mirrors of grace to others, reflecting what we have received ourselves. This implements the Golden Rule in practical terms.

Forgiveness is not a private matter but a corporate one. The body of Christ is a group of people who live daily in the context of forgiveness. What distinguishes us is the fact that we are forgiven sinners. Jesus calls attention, not only to the horizontal elements in the petition, but also to the vertical. We are to pray every day for the forgiveness of our sins.

Some may ask at this point, "If God has already forgiven us, why should we ask for forgiveness? Isn't it wrong to ask for something He's already given us?" The ultimate answer to questions like this is always the same. We do it because God commands it. First John 1:9 points out that one mark of a Christian is his continual asking for forgiveness. The verb tense in the Greek indicates an ongoing process. The desire for forgiveness sets the Christian apart. The unbeliever rationalizes his sinfulness, but the Christian is sensitive to his unworthiness. Confession takes up a significant portion of his prayer time.

Personally, I find it a bit frightening to ask God to forgive us to the extent we forgive others. It's almost like asking God for justice. I used to warn my students: "Don't ask God for justice. You just might get it." If God, in fact, forgave me in *exact proportion* to my willingness to forgive others, I would be in deep trouble.

The mandate to forgive others as we have been forgiven applies also to the matter of self-forgiveness. We have God's promise that when we confess our sins to Him, He will forgive us. Unfortunately, we don't always believe that promise. Confession requires humility on two levels. The first level is the actual admission of guilt; the second level is the humble acceptance of pardon.

A woman distraught about a guilt problem once came

to me and said: "I've asked God to forgive me of this sin over and over, but I still feel guilty. What can I do?" The situation did not involve the multiple repetition of the same sin, but the multiple confession of a sin committed once.

"You must pray again and ask God to forgive you," I replied. A look of frustrated impatience came into her eyes. "But I've done that!" she exclaimed. "I've asked God over and over again to forgive me. What good will it do to ask Him again?"

In my reply, I applied the proverbial firm force of the board to the head of the mule: "I'm not suggesting that you ask God to forgive you for that sin. I'm asking you to seek forgiveness for your arrogance."

The woman was incredulous. "Arrogance? What arrogance?" She was assuming that her repeated entreaties for pardon were proof positive of her humility. She was so contrite over her sin that she felt she had to repent for it forever. She thought her sin was too great to be pardoned by one dose of repentance. Let others get by on grace; she was going to suffer for her sin no matter how gracious God was. Pride had fixed a barrier to this woman's acceptance of forgiveness. When God promises us that He will forgive us, we insult His integrity when we refuse to accept it. To forgive ourselves after God has forgiven us is a duty as well as a privilege.

Lead Us Not into Temptation,
But Deliver Us from Evil

At first glance, this section of the Lord's Prayer seems to be two separate petitions, but that is not the case. It follows the literary form of parallelism used in the Old Testament—two different ways of saying the same thing. Jesus is not suggesting that God will tempt us to evil if we do not petition Him otherwise. James 1:13 specifically says that God tempts no one. God may test, but He never tempts to evil. A test is for growth; temptation is toward evil.

Not all temptation is from Satan, for James also says that we are tempted by our own lust. The evil inherent within the heart of man is capable of tempting man without Satan's help.

The plea to avoid temptation and the petition for deliverance from evil are one and the same. The King James Version is not the best translation of this text, because the evil of which Jesus speaks is not evil in the general sense. In Greek, the word translated as "evil" is neuter in gender; in this section of the Lord's Prayer, the word is masculine in gender. Jesus was saying that we should ask the Father to deliver us from the *Evil One,* from onslaughts Luther called the "unbridled assaults of Satan," the enemy who would destroy the work of Christ in this world.

Jesus was telling us to ask the Father to build a hedge around us. The petition is not designed to avoid the trials of this world, but to protect us from naked exposure to the attacks of Satan. In His "High Priestly Prayer," Jesus asked the Father not to take His disciples out of the world, but rather to "keep them from the evil one [*poneros*]" (John 17:15).

In this petition, we ask for God's redemptive presence. Without that presence, we are easy prey for the enemy. Think of Peter, when he had finished rhapsodizing to Jesus about the extent of his commitment, the depth of his love and devotion, and the intensity of his loyalty. Looking at him and foretelling his denial, Jesus said, "Simon, Simon, behold, Satan demanded to have you, that he might sift you like wheat, but I have prayed for you that your faith may not fail" (Luke 22:31–32). In other words, Jesus told Peter that on his own he would be putty in the hands of Satan. Were it not for the intercession of Christ on Peter's behalf, Peter would have been lost; his faith would have failed.

Not only do we have Jesus to intercede for us to protect us from the enemy, but we ourselves are to ask God to keep us safe from the enemy's hand.

In six petitions, Jesus outlined the pattern and the priorities for our prayer lives. The traditional close of the Lord's

Prayer—"for yours is the kingdom and the power and the glory, forever. Amen"—is not in the best manuscripts. In all probability, it was not in the original text, but was a common conclusion for prayers in the early church. However, it is a fitting and truthful ending. It hearkens back to the prayer's opening, raising a doxology to the One who hears our petitions.

Chapter Four

The Practice
of Prayer

T he Lord's Prayer was given to the church in response
to the disciples' request that Jesus teach them to pray.
In the masterful example of the Lord's Prayer, we see the
priorities of prayer. We also can detect a pattern of prayer,
a fluid movement that begins with adoration and moves
finally to petition and supplication.

The acrostic "A-C-T-S" is useful as a pattern for prayer.
Each letter in the acrostic represents a vital element of
effective prayer:

A — ADORATION
C — CONFESSION
T — THANKSGIVING
S — SUPPLICATION

The complete acrostic suggests the dynamic dimension of prayer. Prayer is action. While it may be expressed in a spirit of serene quietness, it is action, nevertheless. When we pray, we are not passive observers or neutral, detached spectators. Energy is expended in the exercise of prayer.

The Bible tells us that it is the "effectual *fervent* prayer of a righteous man that availeth much" (James 5:16, KJV, emphasis added). Fervency characterized Jesus' agony in Gethsemane, where His sweat fell to the ground as droplets of blood. Fervency describes Jacob's all-night wrestling match with the angel at Peniel. Prayer is an exercise of passion, not of indifference.

Jesus told the parable of the persistent widow taking her case to an unjust judge. The judge, an unscrupulous man with no regard for man or for God, heard the widow's pleas. He was not moved by a sudden burst of compassion, but rather was worn out by her repeated entreaties. In short, the woman became a pest, driving the judge to action by her relentless nagging.

The point of the parable is not that God is indifferent to our needs and must be nagged if we are to be heard. It is not a question of a parallel between the unjust judge and God, the perfectly just Judge. It is a contrast. Jesus frequently uses the "how much more" motif in His parables. Here He states, "And will not God give justice to his elect, who cry to him day and night?" (Luke 18:7). The point of comparison/contrast is this: If an unjust human judge will hear the petition of a fervent woman, *how much more* will our just heavenly Judge hear our petitions?

The persistent woman is likened to the saints who *cry* day and night. Like King David, whose pillow was saturated with his tears, the saints come to God with genuine emotion, even with tears.

Fervency is an appropriate element of active prayer. Frenzy is not. A fine line exists between the two. Both possess passion; both are loaded with emotion. Fervency crosses over into frenzy at two points: the mental and the emotional. Fervency becomes frenzy when the mind stops thinking and the emotions slip out of control. The frenzied prayer lapses into the incoherence of the whirling dervish, and God is not honored.

Frenzy, the counterfeit of fervency, is a contrived attempt

to simulate godly fervor. Those who deliberately manipulate people's emotions are served warning here. There is something holy, something sovereign, about genuine spiritual fervor that cannot be manufactured artificially. It is easy to confuse frenzy and fervor, but the confusion is deadly.

Adoration

As in the pattern of the Lord's Prayer, the most appropriate way to begin prayer is with adoration. Sadly, we are most often moved to prayer by our desires and needs. We go to God when we want something from Him. We are in such a hurry to mention our requests and articulate our needs (which God already knows) that we omit adoration altogether or skip over it quickly in a perfunctory manner.

To omit adoration is to cut the heart out of prayer. It is one thing to be fervent in supplication, particularly while praying in a foxhole; it is another thing to be fervent in adoration. The prayers of the great saints, the prayer warriors of church history, are marked by their fervent adoration of God.

God forbid that we should ever second-guess the teaching of Christ, but I must confess to being at least mildly surprised by Jesus' response to the disciples' request about prayer. When they said, "Teach us to pray," I would have anticipated a different response from His lips than the one He gave by way of the Lord's Prayer. I would have anticipated a response something like this: "Do you want to learn how to pray? Read the Psalms."

I'm surprised Jesus didn't refer the disciples to the Psalms. There we find not only the heart of David exposed, but also a divinely inspired treasury of adoration filled with models for us to follow.

Our hesitancy and weakness in expressing adoration may have two root causes. The first is our simple lack of suitable vocabulary. We tend to be inarticulate when it comes to adoration. It was Edgar Allan Poe who said that prose is a more fitting vehicle to communicate instruction than poetry. The aim of poetry is to lift the soul to lofty heights. It is no wonder the Psalms were written in poetic form. Here the loftiest heights of verbal expression are reached in the service of the soul's praise for God.

Many people in the charismatic movement have declared that one of the chief reasons for their pursuit of the gift of tongues is a keen desire to overcome or bypass the deficiency of an impoverished vocabulary by way of a special prayer language. People often feel their own language is inadequate to express adoration. This sense of inadequacy from having to use the same tired, haggard words yields frustration. A similar view is expressed by Charles Wesley in his hymn "O for a Thousand Tongues to Sing." The hymn complains that the restriction to one tongue is a lamentable hindrance to praise, to be relieved only by the addition of nine hundred and ninety-nine other tongues.

The Psalms were written in simple but powerful vocabulary through which the hearts of several writers expressed reverence for God *without bypassing the mind.* Opening their mouths, the psalmists uttered praise. That praise was given under the inspiration of the Holy Spirit to be sure, but by men whose minds were steeped in the things of God.

Another great barrier to articulate praise is ignorance. We suffer not so much from a limited vocabulary as from a limited understanding of the One whom we are adoring. Our worship also suffers from a lack of knowledge of God.

Consider the love-struck teenager who writes love notes to his girlfriend during study hall. The youth may be shy and reticent, but give him a pen and time to reflect on the object of his romance, and suddenly he is another Shakespeare. Oh, the love notes may be maudlin and less than sophisticated from a literary standpoint, but there is no lack of words. The boy is in love. His heart moves his pen.

How does one pen love letters to an unknown God? How do the lips form words of praise to a nebulous, unnamed Supreme Being? God is a person, with an unending personal history. He has revealed Himself to us not only in the glorious theater of nature, but also in the pages of sacred Scripture. If we fill our minds with His Word, our inarticulate stammers will change to accomplished patterns of meaningful praise. By immersing ourselves in the Psalms, we will not only gain insight into the how of praise, but also enlarge our understanding of the One whom we are praising.

Why should we adore Him? It is our duty as human beings to do so. We have been called to fill the earth with the glory of God. We were created in His image to reflect His glory; our major function is to magnify the Lord. Likewise we are to adore Him, but not to flatter Him, as if to "set Him up" for our supplications. We note that the angels in heaven are described as surrounding the throne of God with praise and adoration.

Why is adoration so important to us in practical terms? Because the whole life of the Christian—which is to be a life of obedience and service—is motivated and enriched when holiness and the dignity of God are etched into our minds. Before I can be motivated to do something difficult for someone, I need to have a certain amount of respect for that person. When someone asks me to go out into the world and endure persecution and hostility from angry and contrary people, I have to respect that person deeply. Only then does that task become easier.

When we begin our prayers with adoration, we are setting the tone for coming to God in confession, in thanksgiving, and in supplication. Hebrews 4:16 tells us that we are to enter into the Holy of Holies *boldly*, for the veil has been removed by the cross. The sword the angel wielded at the gate to paradise has been removed. Christ has given us access to the Father. Yet if we look at the history of the church, people have kept a respectful distance, thinking that God remained aloof from them. Prayer became so formal that the church and its people reacted with equal intensity in the opposite direction.

Today we have "conversational prayer." Our talking to God goes something like this: "Uh, hi there, God. How's it going? Not going too good for me today, but, uh, you know, you and me, God, we'll make it somehow, huh?" This is a rather casual approach to God. It represents an overreaction to formalism, but it turns out to be the kind of informality that breeds contempt. Designed to eliminate artificiality, it has created the worst kind of artificiality. It is hard to imagine that any created being would have the audacity to speak to God like this in His immediate presence.

God has invited us to come freely into His presence, but we must realize that we are still coming before *God*. When confronted with the Lord God Omnipotent Himself, who would speak as if to a friend at a baseball game? We may come boldly, but never arrogantly, never presumptuously, never flippantly, as if we were dealing with a peer.

When we begin our prayer with adoration and praise, we acknowledge the One to whom we are speaking. The grammar need not be perfect, nor the words lofty and eloquent, but they must reflect the respect and the honor due God. There is a sense in which adoration introduces us into the proper mode by which we confess our sins, give our thanks, and make our supplications.

Several recent books would have us believe that all we have to do is follow certain steps and God will give us whatever we ask. The authors say, in effect, "Follow this procedure or use these specific words and know for certain that God will give in to your requests." That's not prayer; that's magic. That's not faith but superstition. These are gimmicks intended to manipulate the sovereign God. But the one who prays like this forgets the One to whom he is speaking. The sovereign God cannot be manipulated, for He knows the hearts of all who pray to Him. True prayer presupposes an attitude of humble submission and adoration to the Almighty God.

Confession

After expressing adoration, we must come to God with hearts of confession. We have no right to come before God at all, apart from the finished work of Christ. We can make no claim, in and of ourselves, to the ear of God. We have no intrinsic right to His presence. The Scriptures tell us that God is too holy even to look at sin. God delights in the prayers of the righteous, but we are not very righteous in our daily lives. Nevertheless, the God we serve invites us into His presence in spite of our sin.

In our study of the Lord's Prayer, we considered some of the important elements of confession. As the model prayer indicates, confession is to be a normal part of our conversation with God. Confession is not a frivolous matter to be engaged in only at appointed times and dates throughout the year. Confession should be a daily activity for the Christian, whose entire pilgrimage is characterized by the spirit of repentance. The principal reason why confession must be on a daily basis is because our sins against divine law are committed on a daily basis. We do things we ought not to do and leave undone those things God commands us to do. We run up a daily indebtedness before God. Consequently, our daily prayers must include genuine acts of confession.

It is no accident that the Roman Catholic Church elevated the rite of penance to the level of a sacrament. Because the sacrament of penance was at the eye of the tornado of the Protestant Reformation, a backlash of negativism toward penitence set in among Protestants. It was a classic case of overreaction, of "throwing the baby out with the bath water." The Reformers sought not the elimination of repentance and confession, but the reformation of the church's practice of these things.

The Roman Catholic sacrament of penance contains several elements: verbal confession, priestly absolution, and "works of satisfaction." These works of satisfaction may be perfunctory tasks such as saying so many "Hail Marys" or "Our Fathers," or they can be more rigorous acts of penance. The works of satisfaction are designed to accrue "congruous merit" for the penitent Christian, making it fitting for God to restore the grace of justification.

It was this third aspect of the sacrament of penance that created so much controversy in the sixteenth century. The works of satisfaction, in the Reformers' eyes, cast a shadow on the sufficiency and the efficacy of Christ's finished work of satisfaction in our behalf on the cross. The "congruous merit" of which Rome spoke obscured the biblical doctrine of justification by faith alone.

In the controversy over penance, the Protestant Reformers did not repudiate the importance of confession, and they acknowledged that confessing one's sins to another human being is biblical. However, they did challenge the requirement of confession to a priest.

The principle of priestly absolution was not a major issue. The Roman Catholic Church has always taught that the priestly words *Te absolvo* ("I absolve you") find their strength in the promise of Jesus to the church that "whatever you bind on earth shall be bound in heaven, and whatever you loose on earth shall be loosed in heaven"

(Matt. 16:19), granting the spokesmen of the church a right to speak the pardon of Christ to penitent people. The Roman Catholic Church understands that the power to forgive sins does not reside ultimately in the priest. The priest is merely a spokesman for Christ. In practice, the priestly absolution differs very little from the Protestant minister's "assurance of pardon," which is given from pulpits across the land every Sunday.

The apostle John tells us, "If we confess our sins, he is faithful and just to forgive us our sins, and to cleanse us from all unrighteousness" (1 John 1:9, KJV). Here we find the promise of God to forgive our confessed sins. To ignore or to neglect this promise is to steer a perilous course. God commands us to confess our sins and promises to forgive our sins. That we should confess our sins daily is clear. What confession means and what it involves are matters that need some elaboration.

We can distinguish between two kinds of repentance: *attrition* and *contrition*. *Attrition* is counterfeit repentance, which never qualifies us for forgiveness. It is like the repentance of a child who is caught in the act of disobeying his mother and cries out, "Mommy, Mommy, I'm sorry, please don't spank me." Attrition is repentance motivated strictly by a fear of punishment. The sinner confesses his sin to God, not out of genuine remorse but out of a desire to secure a ticket out of hell.

True repentance reflects *contrition*, a godly remorse for offending God. Here the sinner mourns his sin, not for the loss of reward or for the threat of judgment, but because he has done injury to the honor of God.

The Roman Catholic Church uses a prayer of confession called "The Act of Contrition" to express this kind of repentance: "O my God, I am heartily sorry for having offended thee. I detest all my sins because of thy just punishment, but most of all because I have offended thee, O my God, who art all good and deserving of all my love. I firmly resolve, with the help of thy grace, to sin no more and to avoid the near occasion of sin."

This prayer goes beyond attrition, the mere fear of punishment, to a godly sorrow for offending God. Notice that the sinner acknowledges that God is *all good* and deserving of our love. This acknowledgment silences all attempts at self-justification.

The prayer includes a firm statement of resolve not to commit the sin again, a willingness to abandon the evil pattern and to avoid even the occasion of it. A humble recognition of dependence on divine mercy and assistance is also included.

Of course, it is possible to use this prayer in a perfunctory manner, merely reciting it as a formal exercise with no heartfelt remorse. Still, the words of the prayer capture the elements of true contrition.

Contrition has lost much of its meaning in our culture. It is not difficult to convince people that they are sinners, for not one in a thousand is going to say that he is perfect. The common response is: "Sure, I'm a sinner. Isn't everyone? Nobody's perfect." There are few, if any, who claim they are blameless, that they have lived lives of ethical consistency, keeping the Golden Rule in every situation. The rub is in acknowledging the intensity of our sin, the extreme godlessness of our actions. Because we are all sinners and know that we share a common guilt, our confession tends to be superficial, often not characterized by earnestness or a sense of moral urgency.

Psalm 51, a contrite sinner's prayer for pardon, was composed by King David after he committed adultery with Bathsheba. David did not approach God with excuses. He did not ask God to consider the circumstances that produced his sin or the loneliness of his government position. David did not seek to minimize the gravity of his sin in God's presence. There were no rationalizations and no attempts at self-justification, which are so characteristic of guilty people.

David said, "I know my transgressions, and my sin is ever before me . . . you may be justified in your words and blameless in your judgment" (vv. 3–4). In other words, David believed that God was absolutely justified if He gave him nothing but absolute punishment. David exhibited what God has said He will not despise: a broken and contrite heart.

David then pleaded for restoration to God's favor: "Create in me a clean heart, O God, and renew a right spirit within me. Cast me not away from your presence, and take not your Holy Spirit from me. Restore to me the joy of your salvation, and uphold me with a willing spirit" (vv. 10–12). He understood the most crucial element of confession: total dependence on God's mercy. David could not atone for his sins. There was nothing he could do and nothing he could say to undo what he had done. There was no way for him to "make it up to God." David understood what Jesus later made clear—that we are debtors who cannot pay our debts.

Confession is like a declaration of bankruptcy. God requires perfection. The slightest sin blemishes a perfect record. All the "good deeds" in the world cannot erase the blemish and move us from imperfection to perfection. Once the sin has been committed, we are morally bankrupt. Our only hope is to have that sin forgiven and covered through the atonement of the One who is altogether perfect.

When we sin, our only option is repentance. Without repentance there is no forgiveness. We must come before God in contrition. David put it this way: "You will not delight in sacrifice . . . The sacrifices of God are a broken spirit; a broken and contrite heart, O God, you will not despise" (Ps. 51:16–17).

Here, David's profound thoughts reveal his understanding of what many Old Testament figures failed to grasp—that the offering of sacrifices in the temple did not gain merit for the sinner. Sacrifices pointed beyond themselves to the perfect Sacrifice. The perfect atonement was offered by the perfect Lamb without blemish. The blood of bulls and goats does not take away sin. The blood of Jesus does. To avail ourselves of the atonement of Christ, to gain that covering, requires that we come before God in brokenness and contrition. The true sacrifices of God are a broken spirit and a contrite heart.

There was an important element of surprise in David's experience of forgiveness. He had begged God to wash away his sin and to make him clean. In a certain sense, forgiveness must never be a surprise. We should never be surprised when God keeps His word to forgive those who confess their sins. God keeps His promises; man does not. God is the Covenant Maker; we are covenant breakers.

Looking at the issue from another perspective, however, we ought to be surprised *every time* we experience forgiveness. We ought never to take God's mercy and forgiveness for granted, even though we live in a culture that does. It is terrifying to consider the ease with which we take God's grace for granted. I occasionally ask collegians, seminarians, seminary professors, and ministers some questions: "Is God obligated to be loving? Is He bound to show forgiveness and grace?" Again and again their answers are in the affirmative: "Yes, of course, it's God's nature to be loving. He's essentially a God of love. If He didn't show love, He wouldn't be God. If God is God, then He *must* be merciful!"

He *must* be merciful? If God must be merciful, then His mercy is no longer free or voluntary. It has become obligatory. If that is the case, it is no longer mercy but justice.

God is never required to be merciful. As soon as we think God is obligated to be merciful, a red light should flash in our brains, indicating that we are no longer thinking about mercy but about justice. We need to do more than sing "Amazing Grace"—we need to be repeatedly amazed by grace.

Thanksgiving

Thanksgiving must be an integral part of prayer. It should be inseparably related to our petitions of supplication. The Scriptures tell us to come to God and make all of our requests known with thanksgiving. Thanksgiving is an acknowledgment of God and His benefits. In Psalm 103:2, David says, "Bless the Lord, O my soul; and forget not all his benefits."

Ingratitude is a serious matter. The Scriptures have much to say about it. The failure to be grateful is the mark both of the pagan and the apostate.

In Romans 1:21, Paul calls attention to two primary sins of the pagan. He says, "For although they knew God they did not honor him as God or give thanks to him." Honor and thanksgiving may be distinguished, but not separated. God is honored by thanksgiving and dishonored by the lack of it. All that we have and all that we are we owe ultimately to the benevolence of our Creator. To slight Him by withholding appropriate gratitude is to exalt ourselves and debase Him.

The pagan must be distinguished from the apostate. The pagan has never entered into the household of faith. He is a stranger to the covenant community. Idolatry and ingratitude characterize him. An apostate is one who joins the church, becomes a member of the visible covenant community, and then repudiates the church, leaving it for a life of secular indulgence. The apostate is "one who forgets." He has a short memory.

Jesus' encounter with the ten lepers illustrates the importance of thanksgiving. Countless sermons have been preached about the healing of the ten lepers, focusing attention on the theme of gratitude. The thrust of many of these sermons has been that Jesus healed ten lepers, but that only one of them was grateful. The only polite response to such preaching is to call it what it is—nonsense. It is inconceivable that a leper enduring the abject misery he faced daily in the ancient world would not be grateful for receiving instant healing from the dreadful disease. Had he been one of the lepers, even Adolf Hitler would have been grateful.

The issue in the story is not one of *gratitude* but of *thanksgiving*. It is one thing to feel grateful; it is another thing to express it. Lepers were cut off from family and friends. Instant cleansing meant release from exile. We can imagine them deliriously happy, rushing home to embrace their wives and children, to announce their healing. Who would not be grateful? But only one of them postponed his return home and took time to *give* thanks. The account in Luke 17 reads: "Then one of them, when he saw that he was healed, turned back, praising God with a loud voice; and he fell on his face at Jesus' feet, *giving him thanks*. Now he was a Samaritan" (vv. 15–16, emphasis added).

All of our prayers are to include thanksgiving. Like the leper, we must pause, turn back, and give thanks. We are so indebted to God that we can never exhaust our opportunities for expressing gratitude.

Forgetting the benefits of God is also the mark of the immature Christian, one who lives by his feelings. He is prone to a roller-coaster spiritual life, moving quickly from ecstatic highs to depressing lows. In the high moments, he feels an exhilarating sense of God's presence, but he plunges to despair the moment he senses an acute absence of such feelings. He lives from blessing to blessing, suffering the pangs of a short memory. He lives always in the present, savoring the "now" but losing sight of what God has done in the past. His obedience and service are only as strong as the intensity of his last memory of blessing.

If God never grants us another glimpse of His glory in this life, if He never grants us another request, if He never gives us another gift from the abundance of His grace, we still would be obligated to spend the rest of our lives thanking Him for what He already has done. We have already been blessed enough to be moved daily to thanksgiving. Nevertheless, God continues to bless us.

Supplication

Someone once said to me, "With so many people starving, it might be wrong for me to pray for a rug for my living room." Yet the God who cares about the empty stomachs of the world is the same God who cares about empty living rooms. What is important to us may also be important to our Father. If we are not sure about the propriety of our request, we should tell that to God. James 1:5 says, "If any of you lacks wisdom, let him ask God, who gives generously to all without reproach, and it will be given him." The Greek phrase translated "without reproach" literally means "without throwing it back in your face." We don't need to be afraid of the reproach of God, provided we are sincerely seeking His will in a given situation.

Nothing is too big or too small to bring before God in prayer, as long as it is not something we know to be contrary to the expressed will of God as made clear in His Word. It would obviously be quite inappropriate to ask God to make us competent thieves. We must not tempt God as did the man who revealed during a national television interview that he had made a pact with God. He declared that he had promised God that if God were to bless his two brothels, he would spend the rest of his life serving Him.

But what if our prayers seem to go unanswered? Sometimes we feel as if our prayers lack the power to penetrate the ceiling. It is as if our petitions fall on deaf ears, and God remains unmoved or unconcerned about our passionate pleading. Why do these feelings haunt us?

There are several reasons why we are sometimes frustrated in prayer. I will review some of the more important ones:

1. We pray in vague generalities. When all our prayers are either vague or universal in scope, it is difficult for us to experience the exhilaration that goes with clear and obvious answers to prayer. If we ask God to "bless everyone in the world" or to "forgive everyone in town," it is difficult to "see" the prayer answered in any concrete way. Having a broad scope of interest in prayer is not wrong, but if all prayer is so general, then no prayer will have specific and concrete application.

2. We are at war with God. If we are out of harmony with God or in open rebellion toward Him, we can hardly expect Him to turn a benevolent ear toward our prayers. His ear is inclined to those who love Him and seek to obey Him. He turns His ear away from the wicked. Thus, an attitude of reverence toward God is vital to the effectiveness of our prayers.

3. We tend to be impatient. When I pray for patience, I tend to ask for it "right now!" It is not uncommon for us to wait years, indeed decades, for our most sincere petitions to be answered. God is rarely in a hurry. On the other hand, our fidelity to God tends to depend on "prompt and courteous" acts by God. If God tarries,

our impatience gives way to frustration. We need to learn patience, asking God for His peace.

4. We have short memories. It is easy for us to forget the benefits and gifts given by the hand of God. The saint remembers the gifts of God and doesn't require a fresh one each hour to keep his faith intact.

Though God does heap grace upon grace, we should be able to rejoice in God's benefits even if we never receive another benefit from Him. Remember the Lord when you go before Him. He will not give you a stone when you ask Him for bread.

Chapter Five

The Prohibitions of Prayer

Very few prohibitions regarding prayer are found in the Scriptures. In Psalm 66:18, the psalmist David penned these divinely inspired words: "If I had cherished iniquity in my heart, the Lord would not have listened." The Hebrew verse could also be translated, "If I *had* iniquity in my heart, the Lord would not have heard."

In either case, David is laying down a condition under which his prayer not only would be ineffective but unheard. The Hebrew word translated "cherished" is *raah*, meaning merely "to see." In other words, if I look at my life and see sin and nurture it, my prayers are an exercise in futility.

Does this mean that if sin is present in our lives, God refuses to hear our prayers? No. If this were so, all prayer would be futile. However, if our hearts are hardened in a spirit of impenitence, our prayers are not only futile but a mockery of God.

In Psalm 66, David reminds himself that there is a time when prayer is a presumptuous, arrogant, detestable, and obnoxious deed perpetrated upon the Almighty. This psalm opens with seventeen verses of joy and praise to God for His mighty deeds. Then, suddenly, there appears in verse 18 the grim reminder of how the entire story could have been drastically different. We are alerted to the importance of properly approaching God in prayer. If there is anything worse than not praying, it is praying in an unworthy manner.

Other Scripture references reflect this attitude. Psalm 109:7 suggests that the prayers of wicked men should be counted as sin. John 9:31 specifically states that the Lord does not hear sinners. Proverbs 15:29 says, "The LORD is far from the wicked, but he hears the prayer of the righteous." Proverbs 28:9 says that the prayer of the disobedient or rebellious is an "abomination" to the Lord. It is disgusting or loathsome to Him.

James, however, tells us that the prayers of *righteous* men accomplish much (5:16). But we are not righteous in our daily lives. Yes, we are clothed with the righteousness of Christ, so that as far as our position before God is concerned, we are righteous. But the practical manifestation of what we are in Christ is sadly inconsistent and woefully inadequate.

Theologians sometimes define a concept by saying what something does *not* say as well as by what it does say. What the psalmist is *not* saying is that if he had been guilty of sin, the Lord would not have heard him. The psalmist is not saying that if he had sin in his heart, God would not have heard him.

Confession Is Integral to Prayer

David is constantly confessing sin in the Psalms. We know that he is not saying that one must be holy in order to pray; otherwise, no one would ever pray. In fact, being a sinner is one of the prerequisites for entrance into the kingdom of God. Jesus said that He did not come to call the righteous, but sinners, to repentance. Looking again to the Lord's

Prayer as a pattern, we note that confession is an integral part of prayer. Without the confession of sin, says 1 John 1:9, there is no forgiveness of sin.

My mentor, Dr. John Gerstner, told of an occasion at one of his meetings when a woman announced to him that she had not sinned for more than twenty years. Dr. Gerstner said that he felt sorry for her because that could only mean she had not prayed in more than twenty years, at least not in the way the Lord told us to pray.

I am not suggesting that the more we sin, the more qualified we are for prayer; that obviously would be a false conclusion. But confessing sin, asking for forgiveness of our "debts" or "trespasses," is an integral part of the practice of prayer, as outlined by our Lord Himself. In fact, the more godly we are, the more devout we will strive to be and the more painfully aware of our sin we will be. It is much the same as walking toward a mountain. The closer we get to that mountain, the bigger it appears.

Think about the fairy tale "The Princess and the Pea." The princess had been gone for some time, and many had tried to lay claim to her throne. To prove true royalty, a scheme was concocted. Many mattresses were stacked on top of one another, with one small pea hidden far down the stack. None of the false princesses had any notion that anything was there, but the true princess could not sleep because of the extreme discomfort the pea gave her. She was extraordinarily sensitive to the presence of the tiny pea.

The lesson for Christians should be clear. When we have that kind of sensitivity to sin, we have royal sensitivity. The closer we are to God, the more the slightest sin will cause us deep sorrow.

We can be sure that being guilty of sin does not disqualify us from the privilege of coming into God's presence. The psalmist is not talking about committing sin, but *allowing* for it. The Puritans spoke of this concept of allowing for sin. It is not so much the victory over sin we need to look at as it is the battle itself. We are in a battle with sin constantly, and we never emerge unscathed.

One of the marks of a true Christian is that he never quits fighting. He doesn't always win, though he will win the ultimate battle because of Christ. If a person ever does give up the fight, then he has truly embraced the evil, legitimizing it. In short, he condones it, even allows it.

In a sermon on the first beatitude, "Blessed are the poor in spirit," the great English preacher Charles Haddon Spurgeon said that "the proud sinner wants Christ, and his own parties; Christ, and his own lusts; Christ, and his own waywardness. The one who is truly poor in spirit wants only Christ, and he will do anything, and give anything to have him!" This is what Psalm 66 is suggesting. The very idea of a person trying to pray while cherishing some sin, while holding on to a sin he is not willing to relinquish to the lordship of Christ, casts a dark shadow of doubt on the validity of his sonship.

Allowing No "Hindrances"

Scripture cites other practical applications of this concept. First Peter 3:7 says: "Likewise, husbands, live with your wives in an understanding way, showing honor to the woman as the weaker vessel, since they are heirs with you of the grace of life, so that your prayers may not be hindered." The Greek word translated "hindered" is *egkoptō*, which literally means "cut off." If discord in the marital relationship is not dealt with, prayers are cut off. This echoes the initial warning of Psalm 66.

A second example is found in Matthew 5:23–24: "So if you are offering your gift at the altar and there remember that your brother has something against you, leave your gift there before the altar and go. First be reconciled to your brother, and then come and offer your gift." Here Jesus is saying that if there are unresolved conflicts in our lives, our worship is blemished. He is setting down priorities. First, we are to give heed to those things that require attention; then we are to come and offer our worship. Though the passage does not speak specifically of prayer, the principle of settling accounts is constant.

When we petition God with unconfessed—hence unpurged—sin lurking in our hearts, we are like the irate college student who confronted his professor about a failing grade. The professor listened politely to the student's frustrations, but remarked that, in his honest professional estimation, the student had received the grade he deserved. The student countered that not only he but also several others in the class felt it was unfair.

The professor, with understandably aroused curiosity, asked what they thought should be done. To that, the student explained: "They've decided that you should be shot. But there's one small problem. Not one of them owns a gun." The professor breathed a sigh of relief and expressed his deepest regret over the "plight" of these students. "But *you* own a gun," the young man said. This student then had the audacity to ask the kindly professor whether he could borrow the professor's own gun so that the students might shoot him.

In a similarly audacious manner, if we see iniquity in our lives and harbor it in our hearts when we pray, we are asking God for the strength we need to curse Him. We are petitioning God for more strength to disobey Him further. Just as the professor was not about to lend his gun to those who would kill him, God is not about to honor our requests made out of sinful hearts.

Chapter Six

The Power
of Prayer

We are moved by the litany of faith that we find in the eleventh chapter of the book of Hebrews. There we have the "Roll Call of Faith," which catalogues the heroic acts of biblical men and women of faith. Their acts are partly summarized in verses 33 and 34: "Who through faith conquered kingdoms, enforced justice, obtained promises, stopped the mouths of lions, quenched the power of fire, escaped the edge of the sword, were made strong out of weakness, became mighty in war, put foreign armies to flight."

The Scriptures do not provide a similar catalogue of the heroes of prayer, but such a list could be compiled easily. Using the same format as does the writer of Hebrews, let us examine a partial list of the accomplishments of prayer:

- By prayer, Esau's heart was changed toward Jacob, so that they met in a friendly, rather than hostile, manner (Gen. 32).

- By the prayer of Moses, God brought the plagues upon Egypt and then removed them again (Ex. 7–11).

- By prayer, Joshua made the sun stand still (Josh. 10).

- By prayer, when Samson was ready to perish with thirst, God brought water out of a hollow place for his sustenance (Judg. 15).

- By prayer, the strength of Samson was restored. He pulled down the temple of Dagon on the Philistines, so that those whom he killed as he died were more than all he had killed in his life (Judg. 16).

- By prayer, Elijah held back the rains for three and a half years. Then by prayer, he caused it to rain again (1 Kings 17–18).

- By the prayer of Hezekiah, God sent an angel and killed in one night 185,000 men in Sennacherib's army (2 Kings 19).
- By the prayer of Asa, God confounded the army of Zerah (2 Chron. 14).

Time would fail me to tell of Abraham, who prayed for and received a son at the age of one hundred years; and Moses, who received help at the Red Sea; and the Israelites, who were delivered from Egypt after much prayer; and David, who escaped the treachery of Saul by prayer; and Solomon, who received great wisdom as the result of prayer; and Daniel, who was able to interpret dreams after prayer. People were delivered from peril, healed from diseases, saw loved ones cured, and witnessed innumerable miracles as the result of fervent prayer.

James, if anything, was understating the case when he wrote that the effective prayer of a righteous man can accomplish much (5:16).

Conditions of the Promises

The power of prayer is neither automatic nor magical. Conditions are attached to the promises of the Bible regarding prayer. At times, Jesus uses a kind of "shorthand," delivering brief aphorisms about prayer to encourage His people in its practice. We are reminded of statements such as, "Ask, and it will be given you" (Matt. 7:7); "If two of you agree on earth about anything they ask, it will be done for them by my Father in heaven" (Matt. 18:19); and, "Whatever you ask in prayer, you will receive, if you have faith" (Matt. 21:22).

Shorthand summaries such as these have provoked bizarre theories of prayer. These happen when people isolate these passages from everything else Jesus and the Bible say about prayer. Distortions also abound when we approach these aphorisms simplistically. Consider the statement about any two people agreeing. It would not be difficult to find two Christians who agree that ridding the world of war or cancer would be a good idea. However, their prayer in this matter would not automatically accomplish their desire. The Word of God indicates that war and disease will be present at the time of Christ's return. To expect their absolute elimination before the appointed time is to grasp the promises of God prematurely.

We still must suffer the ravages of sin, disease, and death. We entreat God to comfort us, to deliver us, to heal us—but we cannot demand these things in an absolute way.

The idea that God "always wills healing" has been a destructive distortion in the Christian community. The pastoral problems emanating from this are enormous. I was once approached by a young man stricken with cerebral palsy. His Christian faith was vibrant, his attitude was contagious with pleasant optimism, and his productivity was exceptional. He had graduated from college with a superior record. His question to me was poignant: "Dr. Sproul, do you think I am possessed by demons?" The question was accompanied by tears. The man's life had been hurled into chaos.

Aghast at this question, I replied, "Why would you even ask such a question?"

The young man proceeded to relate a series of events triggered by an encounter with some Christian friends who had "claimed" the promise of Scripture and "agreed" that the young man be healed of cerebral palsy. They had laid hands on him, praying "the prayer of faith" and claiming a healing for him. When it was apparent that he had not been healed, they first chastised him for his lack of faith. Next they claimed he was guilty of some heinous secret sin that was blocking the healing. Finally they concluded that he was possessed by demons and left him with a tortured soul. His "friends" never considered that the error might be their own. They had given the impression of being zealous, Spirit-filled Christians. Their actions revealed, at best, immaturity; at worst, arrogance and presumption.

Prayer is not magic. God is not a celestial bellhop ready at our beck and call to satisfy our every whim. In some cases, our prayers must involve travail of the soul and agony of heart such as Jesus Himself experienced in the Garden of Gethsemane. Sometimes the immature Christian suffers bitter disappointment, not because God failed to keep His promises, but because well-meaning Christians made promises "for" God that God Himself never authorized.

The simple summaries Jesus gives are designed to encourage us to pray. The pattern seems simple. We are to ask and we will receive. However, the New Testament expands on the conditions, giving us a fuller view of what is involved in effective prayer:

1. John 9:31—"We know that God does not listen to sinners, but if anyone is a worshiper of God and does his will, God listens to him."

2. John 14:13—"Whatever you ask in my name, this I will do, that the Father may be glorified in the Son."

3. John 15:7— "If you abide in me, and my words abide in you, ask whatever you wish, and it shall be done for you."

4. 1 John 3:22—"Whatever we ask we receive from him, because we keep his commandments and do what pleases him."

5. 1 John 5:14—"This is the confidence that we have toward him, that if we ask anything according to his will he hears us."

As these passages reveal, there is more to receiving what we desire from God than the mere asking. Trust in God is not enough. There must be proper reverence for God, obedience to His will, and an ongoing communion with Christ. The request must be made in accordance with the revealed will of God, and in accordance with His nature and character.

The Bible enjoins us to pray "in the name of Jesus." The invoking of Jesus' name is not a magical incantation; its significance lies deeper. In the culture in which the Bible was written, a person's name indicated his attributes and character. To ask for something in Jesus' name is not to add a phrase at the end of a prayer. Rather, it means that we believe that our request is directed to our Great High Priest, our Intercessor.

We have seen that there are certain prerequisites we must follow as we pray. If we ask anything, we must trust in God, knowing that our request is in accordance with the will of the Father and the nature and purpose of Christ. We must have a proper reverence for God as well as the assurance that we are being obedient to what He has revealed to us. We must maintain continuous (albeit imperfect) communion with Christ. After all prerequisites have been met, we may have confidence that our prayers will be answered. The crucial thing to notice is that if we meet these prerequisites, we will not ask for anything outside the will of God.

Another reason our prayers are not always answered as we desire is given to us in James 4:3. We are told that we don't have what we ask because we ask with improper motives, asking in prayer for things that would allow us to pursue wicked pleasures. God is not going to give us things we would misuse. Neither is He going to answer requests made in ignorance, which would prove disastrous.

Moses is a prime example. In Exodus 33:18, he prays, "Please show me your glory." Moses has talked with God. He has seen God do numerous miracles: the burning bush, the plagues, the parting of the Red Sea. But now Moses wants the big one: "God, those other things were great, but now let me have it all. Let me see your face!"

In verses 19 and 20, God says: "I will make all my goodness pass before you and will proclaim before you my name 'The LORD.' And I will be gracious to whom I will be gracious, and will show mercy on whom I will show mercy. But . . . you cannot see my face, for man shall not see me and live."

God was doing Moses a monumental favor by refusing to honor his request. If God had granted Moses his wish, it would have cost him his life. No man can see God and live. Moses should have rejoiced that God said no.

Another reason that we fail to see the desired answers to our prayers may be because we are praying for things we already have in Christ. In John 4, Jesus speaks with the woman at the well. He tells her that if she realized to whom she was speaking, she would have known what to request. The same is true of us. If we really knew who God is and all that He has given us in Christ, our prayer lives would be far different from what they are.

The Power of the Intercessor

Prayer is the priestly function of carrying a petition to God. In Old Testament times, two major classes of mediators functioned between God and His people: prophets and priests. Stated simply, the prophet was ordained by God to speak His divine Word to the people. The prophet spoke to the people for God. Conversely, the priest was ordained by God to be a spokesman for the people. The priest spoke to God for the people.

In the New Testament, Christ exercises the offices not only of Prophet and Priest but of King. In His priestly role, He made the perfect sacrifice, offering the perfect atonement once and for all. Yet the cross was not the end of Christ's priestly office. In His ascension He entered the heavenly Holy of Holies, where He continues to act as our Great High Priest. There He prays for His people, interceding with the Father on our behalf. The power of Christ's prayers is immeasurable. It can be illustrated not only by the miracles He performed on earth, but also by His prayers of intercession during His earthly ministry.

Consider the cases of Judas and Simon Peter. Both were disciples who had committed heinous acts of treachery against Jesus in His darkest hour. Judas committed suicide, whereas Simon was restored and became the "Rock" of the early church in Jerusalem. Why?

One critical difference between these men may be seen in Jesus' announcements of their forthcoming treachery. About Judas He said, "Truly, truly, I say to you, one of you will betray me" (John 13:21). When the disciples asked Jesus to identify the traitor, He replied, "It is he to whom I will give this morsel of bread when I have dipped it" (v. 26). Then Jesus dipped the morsel, gave it to Judas, and said, "What you are going to do, do quickly" (v. 27).

Later that evening in His great prayer of intercession, Jesus said: "While I was with them, I kept them in your name, which you have given me. I have guarded them, and not one of them has been lost except the son of destruction, that the Scripture might be fulfilled" (John 17:12). Here Jesus prayed *about* Judas, but not *for* Judas, and called him the "son of destruction."

In the case of Peter's denial, Jesus announced to him: "Simon, Simon, behold, Satan demanded to have you, that he might sift you like wheat, but I have prayed for you that your faith may not fail. And when you have turned again, strengthen your brothers" (Luke 22:31–32).

Notice that Jesus did not say, "If you have turned again,

strengthen your brothers," but "when you have turned." Jesus was confident of Peter's restoration. We cannot help but draw the conclusion that Jesus' confidence was in large measure due to His earlier words: "but I have prayed for you."

Jesus prayed *about* Judas. He prayed *for* Simon Peter. He made intercession for Peter. He acted as Peter's priest. At this very moment Christ is acting as our High Priest, interceding for us.

This is the jubilant conclusion of the author in Hebrews 4:14–16:

> Since then we have a great high priest who has passed through the heavens, Jesus, the Son of God, let us hold fast our confession. For we do not have a high priest who is unable to sympathize with our weaknesses, but one who in every respect has been tempted as we are, yet without sin. Let us then with confidence draw near to the throne of grace, that we may receive mercy and find grace to help in time of need.

May these words become life to our souls as we appropriate them for ourselves.

Tapping into Prayer's Power

Prayer requires structure, but not at the expense of spontaneity. I have tried to give direction to avoid harmful pitfalls in our pilgrimage. No band director tells his musicians to play whatever is on their hearts and then expects to hear "The Star-Spangled Banner." There must be order, and the procedure must be somewhat regulated. However, room still exists for individual self-expression within the limits of reverence and order.

Why do we pray?

- We pray because God has commanded it and because He is glorified when we pray.
- We pray because it prepares our hearts for what we will receive from Him.
- We pray because much is accomplished by prayer.
- We pray to adore God, to praise Him, to express our wonder at His majesty, His sovereignty, and His mighty acts.
- We pray to confess to God our sins, numerous as they are, and to experience grace, mercy, and forgiveness at His hand.
- We pray to thank Him for all that He is and all that He has done.

- We pray to make our supplication known to Him, to fulfill the invitation He has left us.

When we pray, we must remember who God is and who we are before Him. We must remember first and foremost that God's name is to be kept holy. We must remember that He is the Source of our provision and that all good things come from Him. We are to live in such a way that we make visible the kingdom of God in this world. We must regularly confess our sin, for that is one of the surest marks of a Christian. We are to pray that God will protect us from the evil one.

We must always remember that God is God and owes no man anything. As the psalmist says, "He does all that he pleases" (Ps. 115:3). We have been invited to come boldly before God, but never flippantly, arrogantly, or presumptuously. Ecclesiastes 5:2 reminds us that we are not to be "hasty to utter a word before God, for God is in heaven, and you upon the earth."

Finally, if there is a secret to learning how to pray, it is no different from that of any other endeavor. To become accomplished in anything, we must practice. If we want to learn how to pray, then we must pray—and continue to pray.

About the Author

Dr. R.C. Sproul was founder of Ligonier Ministries, founding pastor of Saint Andrew's Chapel in Sanford, Fla., first president of Reformation Bible College, and executive editor of *Tabletalk* magazine. His radio program, *Renewing Your Mind*, is still broadcast daily on hundreds of radio stations around the world and can also be heard online. He was author of more than one hundred books, including *The Holiness of God*, *Chosen by God*, and *Everyone's a Theologian*. He was recognized throughout the world for his articulate defense of the inerrancy of Scripture and the need for God's people to stand with conviction upon His Word.

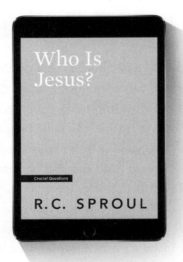

ASK LIGONIER

Do we have free will?

Is it true that God controls everything?

Does prayer change things?

A Place to Find Answers

Maybe you're leading a Bible study tomorrow. Maybe you're just beginning to dig deeper. It's good to know that you can always ask Ligonier. For more than fifty years, Christians have been looking to Ligonier Ministries, the teaching fellowship of R.C. Sproul, for clear and helpful answers to biblical and theological questions. Now you can ask those questions online as they arise, confident that our team will work quickly to provide clear, concise, and trustworthy answers. The *Ask Ligonier* podcast provides another avenue for you to submit questions to some of the most trusted pastors and teachers who are serving the church today. When you have questions, just ask Ligonier.

FOR MORE INFORMATION, VISIT ASK.LIGONIER.ORG